Trojan Gifts

Trojan Gifts

Mark Mahemoff

PUNCHER & WATTMANN

First published in 2022
Published by Puncher & Wattmann
PO Box 279
Waratah NSW 2298

info@puncherandwattmann.com

NATIONAL
LIBRARY
OF AUSTRALIA

ISBN   9781922571366

Cover design by David Musgrave

Printed by Lightning Source International

This project has been assisted by the Australian Government through the Australia Council, its arts funding and advisory body.

Australian Government

Australia Council
for the Arts

Contents

Ted Bundy explains: a found poem

"You can go to the mouth of any great river
and pull out a handful of water
that's flowing from it and say,
where did it come from?

To trace it back, okay,
and this is what we're dealing with here,
we're talking about microscopic events,
as it were,
and undistinguishable, undetectable events.

The melting of a single snowflake,
as it were, okay?
The advent of spring,
and the combination of other forces
perhaps,
and the ultimate, uh, result
that we appreciate
which is the river itself."

From the telemovie series, "Conversations with a Killer: The Ted Bundy
Tapes". (Creator: Joe Berlinger, 2019)

Bridgework

She studies that old photo of a young couple
preserved in the amber of their past happiness,
the palpable elation of infatuation,
a glass of wine in their hands,
and the certainty those feelings
would never diminish.

But love is deciduous
and prey to weather's vagaries.

In recent days they sit apart on their couch
the way some married couples
end up sleeping separately.

The silence between them
is filled with a need
that neither one has worked out
how to satisfy or quell.

At times they find themselves
bridging this gulf
with soft words
as if to resuscitate a truth.

Glebe Fair

The relentless rain has suddenly relented.
It's early summer, the crowd is small.
Stalls are selling scratched LPs,
gözleme, hemp shirts and thirdhand books.

A guy with dreads
sings his sweet, Gen Z version
of Father and Son
against a backdrop which includes
an overcast sky
and trees with star shaped leaves.

An elderly couple eat nachos from paper plates
while we all weakly applaud his Creedence cover.

No one buys a copy of his $10 CD,
not because it's not good,
but because it's not good enough
to just be good
when one's competition
is the ambience of unleased shops
and graffiti streaked windows
in a warm and cloudy Sydney
with the odd raindrop descending,
heavy as a grape.

Memory's territory

10 years old
on my King of The Road scooter.
Its red enamel frame
and white, pneumatic tyres
absorbed most shocks
as I zoomed from the local shops
down childhood's winding path.
*

Adolescent on a skateboard
with orange deck
and green, translucent wheels.
I took exquisite risks,
then slowed down
using driveways like
runaway truck ramps,
and came to an elegant stop
in front of my house.
*

Those worlds, now extinct,
were entirely of my making.
Dangerous and free.
Memory's territory.

Bachelor

Observe the stack of pizza boxes
in a corner, growing fur.
Almost empty coffee mugs
resting on their rings.
A platoon of cockroaches
rallying in the kitchen.
A recently constructed flat pack cupboard
with four screws left unused.

Note the fridge's mosaic of magnets
advertising plumbers, handymen
and tree loppers
while an ominous brown liquid
pools in the crisper drawer.

And reclining in one of three
mismatched lounge chairs
is the occupant, cheerfully childless,
munching snacks from a cardboard box
with, he thinks, all the time in the world.

Trojan gifts

Soon after meeting they were in each other's arms
seeking asylum and singular comfort.
All that existed was the present and its gifts.
The past was a blemish they were trying to erase.
Before long they cohabited to craft a different life.
It seemed then their beginning would never have an end.

They held too much confidence to contemplate an end.
Who could know one day she'd snub the safety of his arms.
Many years were spent constructing a good life,
a future which contained uninterrupted comfort.
They both felt it crucial that neither one erase
their haven before sharing the joy of common gifts.

Accrued acts of betrayal segue into "Trojan gifts"
which suddenly reveal themselves, hastening the end.
One can always choose to sooth and erase
hurt and frustration in someone else's arms.
But they hadn't yet sought this ultimate cold comfort,
the snare within the warmth of another stranger's life.

Some say the fence's other side portrays a burnished life
or what appears to be an array of gleaming gifts.
Relationships are tested by unforeseen discomfort,
unimagined ruptures miscomprehended as the end.
The myth that one finds sanctuary within a stranger's arms
sustains a strong desire which time struggles to erase.

It was easy to fathom but tricky to erase
their contrition at midnight, side by side, facing life.
Always shattering illusions in one another's arms,
they tended to forget their cache of gifts
stockpiled over years, which had hardly reached an end.
Vigilance for danger has a way of ruining comfort

while advancing age increases a hankering for comfort.
There's a drive to rehash anecdotes that protests don't erase.
The cycle of squabble and forgiveness doesn't end
or staunch the flow of uncertainty through life.
What prevented him from grasping her need for poignant gifts?
Why didn't she know all he wanted was her arms?

Still, they recognized the fickleness of life and its gifts,
the need to lay down arms in order to have comfort
and finally erase the fear which only hope can end.

Mundy Park, Vancouver Winter

My first time in below zero weather,
unprepared, with the wrong type of jacket,
the cold is threatening.

Moody and uncomfortable,
I walk alongside children and in-laws,
the Canadian branch of my partner's family,
their warmth and generosity hard to comprehend.

Then suddenly I'm confronted with a frozen lake.
Random upright tree branches paralysed in ice.
I skip a rock across its rink-like surface.
It bounces, slides and halts
like a kid in school socks on varnished floorboards.

Inhaling painful air,
my face becomes a tingling mask.
I look down at dead leaves encrusted with snowflakes.

Pensioners in puffy parkers
walk dogs in woollen vests.
They smile at me like neighbours
I've lived beside for years.

At the end of our tour we head back to Bill's house
where I'm embraced by central heating's welcoming arms.
I'm aware more than ever that I'm in another country
and that I am more at home far away from home.

Sauropods

The sky is grim with clouds as we crawl through Harris Park. It's
only 4 p.m but red and green neon is splashing on footpaths. Fenced
off vacant lots wait for development. Backyards store swing sets
abandoned tricycles and cars. Canals dry just yesterday are streaming
with debris. Our train stops and waits for its signal to get moving.
Out here it's a relentless Meccano set of scaffolding. No one lives
far from the remorselessness of highways. Houses abut industrial
estates. Barbed fences are softened by unkillable lantana. Cranes are
metal sauropods maintaining a vigil. "Last stop Central!" Words
terminate like platforms.

At the Land Registry Office

This place is as grey
as its Heuga carpet tiles.

I'm second in line
and clutch a ticket stub
that proves it.

Soon I'm sitting on a stained chair
at a chipped, white laminex desk
opposite a large, bald bureaucrat
and his yellowing football poster.

He stays silent while I hand him
a small wad of documents.
He peruses them and says,
"Yeah, nah mate, there's something missing."

I surprise myself by suddenly
bursting into laughter.
Somehow, I knew
this wouldn't be straightforward.

"Here mate," he says
and hands me a new form.
"Just fill in the sections
I've marked with an X."

I stare at it blankly
and rifle through my papers,
locating all the details
he must have known were there.

But all roads have led
to this standard government office
in a shabby sandstone edifice
in the middle of the city.

So I take my ticket stub
to cashier 26,
pay the lodgement fee
and commit it all to memory.

Parts of Vietnam

1. Ablutions

Late morning
on a Hoi An street.

The heat slowly rises
as an elderly woman

approaches the riverbank
as if to sit and rest.

Her face is ancient
but she is younger than it looks.

Without any warning
she peels down her pants

and squats discreetly
out of sight of pedestrians.

This quick flash reveals
dried peach buttocks

with a sparse grey tuft
in her bony pelvic cleft.

Slowly, demurely,
she straightens from her haunches,

straddles her bicycle,
and rides into the distance.

2. Eating Dogs

"It's not a topic we like to discuss.
It boils down to a matter of taste.
Yes, they are farmed for that specific purpose.
Chihuahuas for entree, St Bernards for mains.

Let's be honest, a dog, like a chicken, is edible.
Do they deserve more love than a sheep or goat?
But I must admit, I've stopped eating them myself.
Old age seems to have made me sentimental.

It might often be a neighbourhood mongrel.
Sometimes even the family pet.
Yes, kids get upset, but a new one dries their tears.
I'm just kidding, you Caucasians can be so gullible."

Outside Mudgee

An unsealed road
leads to the dam.

Six geese are using
one half as their home.

The other is choked
with lilies and duckweed.

A kangaroo maintains vigilance
some distance from the house.

It's a gaunt-faced sentinel,
voluntary and gentle.

So little is happening,
meaning packs each moment.

A steady downpour, a lowing cow,
tyres on gravel fading towards town.

Casualties

We walk past a homeless man,
his Pit Bull pressed close
and a dented paper cup
pleading for coins.

He's becoming invisible.
Or our ethics are fading.
Either way today
he doesn't get our change.

This amid a multitude of cruelties
we inflict while rushing
to catch a morning train.

Haven

"You seem to know yourself,"
she quipped.

He wanted to know someone else,
someone less constrained, less fragmented,

more able to stay up until 5 a.m.
drinking with a stranger

in a beachside hotel room,
grey clouds a welcome bulwark against sunlight,

only leaving for more booze and food,
both laughing at their lack of certainty,

while waves foam and break
beyond a rusting balcony.

Five Monostiches

Before my grandmother died at 92 she asked if the internet closes on
a Sunday.

*

One's children are never quite old enough for adulthood.

*

She's at home in her own skin, I'm a squatter in mine.

*

The taller my son grows the further away he wants me to stand.

*

My mother's death has helped me make sense of her life.

Dim light

Dark June afternoon.
Cold. Everything chiselled
from dim light.

The city's caught up
in its own affairs.

A busking beatboxer
sounds like a band
equipped with just his mouth,
mic and nerve.

In a pub's front window
an old man is
losing an argument with himself.

At Town Hall station
someone who collapsed
near the ticket booth
is wearing an oxygen mask.

The paramedics look distracted.
Their clean, white latex hands
gently hold
his filthy head still.

Everywhere
no one is listening.

Meat display

His woodblock is a sawn,
unvarnished chunk of tree trunk.
His cleaver, honed steel.
Its handle, an afterthought.

He has hacked through countless limbs,
binned bags of bone fragments,
rendered and stockpiled lard in vats.

To him farm animals
are bereft of sentience.
It's not deliberate cruelty,
just repetition's blindness.

In the street they stand and gawk
at the meat window display.
Sausages dripping and coiled
like the viscera that encases them.

You wrestle with your conscience
before walking in
and request a chopped heap
of something which once breathed.

Homage to grey

Let's paint the town grey,
dim the lighting, drop the volume,
keep the sun's rays at bay.
        Let clouds reign.
Their ersatz softness
so seductive and unreachable:
a salve for grief and loss.
        This morning was perfect greyness
like duco from the 40s.
        Those muted pink and mint sedans
always appeared matt.
Today displays no gloss:
it feels much better for that.
        Let's paint the town grey,
if only for a while.
Red now feels passé.
Grey is back in style.

Floating toys

"Don t throw the baby out
with the bath water," he said.
You heard this cliché literally,
imagined watching
the last tiny foot
as it gurgled
             down the drain.
And those floating toys
marooned near a loofah:
a yellow squeaky duck,
a tugboat:
the remnants of a life.

A drama

Two birds, pigeon-like but elegant,
less insistent, breasts lightly speckled,
land in mint gone wild
near the back fence.

It seems random at first.
Each one turns up alone,
pecking at invisible titbits.

But soon they nuzzle,
fly off and fly back
like a couple immersed
in their first weeks of romance.

Though just as hastily they disperse,
leaving the yard bereft
without their brief,
spontaneous dance.

The message

Childhood disappears in increments.
It begins with watching grandparents.
Old when you're young,
they're aware they're ending.
They've been where you're going
and look back more than forward.
What's ahead for them
is less and dubious.

Maybe a neighbour's pet
is struck down in the street.
Mum and dad might shield you
with words and hugs.
But you cover your eyes
and squint through parted fingers.

If you're lucky you'll survive it
with a kind of immunity.
A kernel of hope harboured
while you wade through adulthood.

Emptied nest

You imagine them gone,
somewhere far away,
conducting their lives
under your radar.
        And sometimes travelling
to see them again
or them to see you,
waiting at the airport or train station,
trying to identify
their faces among hundreds,
then tears and smiles,
hugs and reminiscences.
        And when it's over,
after days or weeks,
each returning to a life
now reinforced as separate,
discrete and disentangled
from the chaffing of proximity.
        Memories precise and cobbled
from compelling fragments
which have brought you
and will bring you
to moments here and now
so slowly, so quickly, so finite.

Proofs

Again, I consider my grandfather,
his crimes bestowed on me as facts.

His death was an event
I could not fully comprehend.

But I'm told by those who knew
that he was feared, scorned and bypassed.

Barely huggable by my father
even when near death.

I recall him as an old, fat man
who joked with his false teeth.

My strongest recollection
is the day of his funeral.

It had rained incessantly
the entire night before.

Sunlight and blue sky
contrasted with thick mud

which all of us tramped through
on our way to his grave.

Bloodwork

"The X-rays are clear.
No shadows. Nothing sinister.
We marked the bloodwork urgent.
Is there anything else you require?"

To feel well, to gain acceptance.
Is that too much to ask?

"I'm sorry. That's life.
There's no cure for it yet.
But we do bulk bill.
What did you expect?"

I expected kindness.
Possibly compassion.

"There are no item numbers
for those specific services.
But here's a feedback form.
And there's the suggestion box."

Our happy place

A specific quietness.
A mountain.
Windows thinly iced each morning.

That was ours alone.

A cola-coloured river.
Old objects restored
to brand new antiqueness.

That was ours alone.

Temperate rainforest.
Moss and lichen.
Everything mollified by foliage.

That was ours alone.

Us inseparable,
as if it couldn't end.

That was ours alone.

A sliver of moon

> Afterwards they lay,
bewildered and angry,
in the inner city's incomplete silence.
> Slats of light
tattooed their nakedness.
They wondered how to clear
their hurdles of incompetence.
> He left the bed,
insubstantial in the darkness.
She waited, crumpled like the sheet
at her feet.
> And before he returned
she got up and stared
through the bathroom window
at a sliver of moon.

Haiku

A secondhand lamp
bent over half-baked poems
struggles to shed light.

For A.

I never imagined you'd be old enough
to leave us behind, smiling with your friends,
healthily ignoring our misgivings,
as if our love is robust enough to snub.
      I realized then how much I needed your neediness,
this person I never believed I could be
or find inside. No, not inside,
more a series of partial renovations
from bachelor, to boyfriend, to spouse
and finally parent; each role an annex,
until at some point they cohered.
      But there's always "me" who stands back,
detached from this rickety construction,
the false starts and doubts
intrinsic to this ongoing project
which I am and you are my daughter,
both of us always becoming what we'll be.

Aspects of Myrtle Street

1.

People place
Early December.
Blazing sky and still heat
rising from a newly laid
liquorice strap black street.

Wangal Nura Park's been dug up.
Bare dirt and random mounds.
Rich soil waiting to be spread.
A green concrete slab
lined up for ball games
and a swing set with slide
are all that's left unrazed.

I point out a flame tree.
Its red bells
almost ring in the humidity.
He loves its intense colour
and snaps off a branch
to take back to mum.

We leave late afternoon and loiter
at a bush with small, mauve flowers.
I tell him to pick one,
remove the green, stopped end
like a tiny cork,
(the way I once did when I was young),
and squeeze his fingers gently
down its stem

to express a small drop of lickable sweetness.
Next we pass a hedge of gardenias
already beginning their swift, brown wilt,
and inhale the rich perfume
while climbing our street's hill,
sweating towards home.

2.

Years later
we return to that reserve.

I'm 54, you're 15
and 6ft tall,
with basketball in hand.

I shoot hoops too
as if I know what I'm doing,
creating a hiatus
within which we practice
being father and son.

You set up a Bluetooth speaker
in the middle of the court.
Spotify plays Hilltop Hoods and AC/DC.
You thank me for passing on my knowledge.
I tell you your grandpa did the same for me.

In the background kids and mums
are packing up to leave
but we remain
until daylight segues into streetlight,
while the concrete relinquishes its heat

and perspiration drips from us
like unexpressed tears.

Wangal Nura translates as "People place" in the Dharug language

A woman with SEAWORLD embroidered on her vest

A woman with SEAWORLD
embroidered on her vest
is sitting on the bus,
immobilised by sadness.

What could have happened
to make her feel this way?
Did her favourite dugong die?
Did the seals stop doing tricks?

And is it fair to link
her affect with her workplace?
I'm at a loss to understand
what's lured me into caring.

She alights before me
but stays on my mind.
When I disembark
my thoughts of her do too.

A woman with SEAWORLD
embroidered on her vest
was sitting on the bus,
immobilised by sadness.

Absence and Presence

At first, whenever he was physically absent,
she yearned for his physical presence.
And whenever she was physically absent
he yearned for hers. They would never tire
of each other's physical presence.
They never experienced
each other's emotional absence.

But incrementally, when he was physically present,
she began to experience him as emotionally absent.
At these times she'd prefer him to be physically absent
so that the pain produced
by her feeling his absence
made sense.

When he was physically present
she wanted him to also be emotionally present.
When he was physically absent
and she was not preoccupied
with her sense of his emotional absence when he was present,
she could at least imagine she might be on his mind,
and in that sense, could feel that she was with him.

But what about his actual state of mind
when he was physically absent
or physically present
or when she experienced him as emotionally absent?
Under those circumstances
he was often reacting to her perceived anger and avoidance,
which (she would have explained this to him if he had ever
bothered to ask)

was her reaction to his perceived withdrawal.

And almost as a form of retribution,
or in order to alleviate his pain and anger
at not understanding her behaviour,
he would continue to withdraw
while in her physical presence.
(He would have explained this to her if she had ever bothered to ask)
.

When he was physically absent
for increasingly extended periods of time
and she'd stopped contacting him
to find out why he was physically absent,
he imagined she'd stopped caring
about his presence or absence,
physical or emotional.

His increasing belief that she no longer cared
about his physical or emotional presence or absence
led to an exponential increase
in his physical and emotional absence.
In time she followed suit.

Their friends observed their increasing absence
from each other physically and emotionally
when in each other's presence or not.
Their friends' opinions were often split along gender lines.

Now, regrettably, when they are both present physically,
they are almost completely absent emotionally
and when absent physically, are almost never
on each other's minds.
But still, in the total privacy of their own minds,
they sometimes reminisce

44

about those years, at the beginning,
when the only thing on their minds
was each other.
They have no intention of ever revealing this.

Kernels

Clouds threaten the washing
you're trying to unpeg
don't wish them away
stay in this moment
hour by hour
day by day

*

Downstairs they're chatting
children starting life
with all its expectations
joys and pains
you know this
or think you do
prone to shutting out
what's new

*

Listen to the morning news
catastrophe is de rigueur
while just meters from your feet
a dog is busy sleeping
unconscious of humanity's
sowing and reaping

*

Tie yourself
to the mast of giving
unlearn the need to hoard
your feelings and goods
your hard-won earnings
suspecting you have more
than most
through luck
not from what hard work brings.

Two phases of summer

The jacaranda's sudden petal eruption
ices cars and spatters streets blue/purple.
The memory of their gorgeousness
outlasts this fleeting flowering
and sad return to nakedness.

*

Yellows, whites and pinks
of frangipani blossoms
emerge with carnal fragrance
and snapped branch white blood
dripping stickily.
Though soon enough
they're mush underfoot.
A skeleton's left standing:
succulent and bare.

Allen Keys

for J.

I've watched him progress
from Lego to IKEA
crayons to Allen Keys

clichés are clichés for a reason
inside each one
is a durable truth

meanwhile he grows past us
like a beanstalk from seeds
we recklessly sowed

Such depths

All it takes is walking
from the bus stop
a mother adjusting
her giggling child's car seat
a poker-faced cat
recumbent on a red brick wall
a nicotine sun as I walk home.

Write yourself through
the crush of this moment
as if it's the last
a woman's floral presence
high heels
a bee-stung pout
there are such depths sometimes.

Autonomy

I was on the M10
heading west to Norton Street
when you noticed him waiting
at the bus stop after school.

I wanted to know
why he hadn't boarded mine.
After all we were both bound
for the same destination.

At his age I remember
longing for autonomy
until I got home
and scoffed mum's afternoon tea.

This boy, my son,
rode inside my thoughts
until he turned up later
and, reassured, I hugged him.

Family members
can feel strange to one another,
sometimes more than actual strangers:
father, mother, sister and brother.

Dorothy once lived on our street

Dorothy was an ex-nun who lived on our street.
She kept track of all the comings and goings.
She seemed content as the local sticky-beak.
She would praise us one day and curse us the next.

She talked to herself, sometimes even shouted.
We could hear her at night, alone in her bedroom,
in heated conversation with an enigmatic past.
Most of us avoided her, some took pity,
fewer still befriended her, completely on her terms.

Then one day, inexplicably, her house became silent.
No one was eager to ask too many questions.

But the void she left behind is palpable with loss.
Her life confronted us with the mess of our existence,
the untidiness most of us try to efface.
Our street was the place that Dorothy once lived.
Dorothy's death now lives here instead.

Candlelight

The power outage
plunged us into a void,
all appliances extinguished,
their distinctive voices curtly gagged.

Our devices left us to our own devices,
bereft, stranded and forgotten,
like living our lives trapped on a raft
drifting off the mainland,
all of us waving madly for attention.

We scrabbled blindly
in cluttered kitchen drawers,
found candles but not matches,
were forced to light their wicks
from the flames of our gas stove.

But when the panic waned
we chatted and laughed,
as if that might actually
be enough to sustain us.

Then the power returned
in a jarring surge,
and again, the TV
blurted out its pig ignorance,
and the lights blared back down
with halogen brutality.

But this time we decided
to switch them off ourselves,
suddenly empowered and enlightened,
content, after all,
to reconnect in darkness.

Barwon Heads

Weatherboard shacks abut
cookie cutter mansions.
On one side of the street
they sell pies and fries,
on the other, wheels of aged cheese
and truffle infused oil.

Late afternoon, on a shady deck,
adjacent to a patchy lawn,
an unused Weber mulls over its future.

Cozzies dry pragmatically
over pinewood dining chairs.
Nameless birds screech at a darkening sky.

Big smoke sarcasm dissipates
as we walk along the lake.
Signs describe the necessity
of nurturing saltmarshes.

Lake Connewarre's planed flat
by the wind's deft carpentry.
Fisherman up early brood,
rods dangling, catching nothing.
Sweaty joggers wheeze a good morning
and shrink into the distance.

Someone called Frank is surfing domain.com.
"This is it honey, I've found our little slice of heaven,"
he declares,
and rushes to the Estate Agent
to put down a holding deposit.

It may or may not be the decision of a lifetime
but he believes it to be
while reclining on his virtual sundeck,
surveying the virtual scenery.

Cinerary facts

Pacemakers and other devices
must be removed.
The body must be contained
in a coffin with a nameplate.
Cremations must happen
one body at a time.

The ashes must be put
into a metal container
and allowed to cool.
They are then loaded
into a homogenizer
to reduce the size of the particles.

In their final state
the ashes are packed
in a plastic container
and the nameplate is attached.
The container is then stored
in a locked room.

When the applicant collects the ashes
they can be buried in a cemetery,
placed in a columbarium,
scattered on private land
or a beach or a river or a public park
or at sea
or in a place that held significance
for the deceased or loved ones.
The applicant must seek permission
for taking up some of these options.

for taking up some of these options.

Once scattered, the ashes cannot be retrieved.

Many of these facts were gathered from the NSW Health website: http://www.health.nsw.gov.au/environment/factsheets/Pages/cremation-ashes.aspx

Funeral home

The director guided a small clutch of the willing to a room in
which her corpse was the centerpiece. Others waited in the hot,
dusty street, afraid of confronting the depth of their loss. Everyone
seemed to float in grief-stricken silence. The shroud was gently
lifted as if taking her feelings into account. The dead face reminded
him that he was still alive.

   After the shock and tears his gaze was diverted by artificial
flowers, a tapestry of the twelve apostles, and an enormous New
Testament on a cheap lectern. Her voice was discernable among
his thoughts. Then he turned again to see her smooth, waxy face.
She looked so terribly slight. He'd always prepared himself for that
moment. The body. The hushed tones. The finality.

   Later, during lunch, they ate, drank, and reminisced. Time's
cool brutality continued its erasures, pushing him forward against
his will.

Lane Cove morning

Thirty years together,
they're now exiting their sixties.

She passes him her new iPad
which he tries to operate.
She grins with resignation
while facing the traffic.

They're settled with each other now.
The kids have grown and left.
A grandchild's on the way.

They spend mornings together again,
a library of experience behind them.

"I love Liz dearly, don't get me wrong,
but I don't like being told
how I should live my life!"

Bytes of monologue
mingle with birds and a barista
bashing out spent coffee grounds.

Are they happy or stoic?
Is the question even necessary?

He listens impassively,
still trying to get
the damn contraption to work.

Raking

On weekends he'd mow and rake,
stubbies faded, the elasticised waist perishing
below a distended belly, builder's cleavage exposed,
shirtless, back sopping in the midday sun.

On weekdays it was suit and tie,
5 a.m. starts,
his car slowly backing down the driveway
into darkness.

This treadmill trundled on for years.
Frustration morphing into anger,
then indifference.
Everyone stewing in private hells.

Decades on it appears to be forgotten.
Garden, lawn, house and rake gone.
Marriage over, children grown.
A fresh mulch of denial spread thickly each season.

Pillow

Late afternoon up north is hot
and loud with the tinnitus of insects.
You know you've nodded off
when a book falls from your hands.

At night your pillow
is damp as a sickbed.
The soil as dry
as a sloughed cicada shell.

You perch in darkness
on the edge of your mattress,
hoping sleep arrives
before morning does.

On the Daintree River

At 4 p.m. Ray greets us smiling, tattooed from neck to ankles.
It turns out he knows a bit about crocodiles.

"Ray, what do crocodiles eat?"

"Mate, they eat whatever they bloody well want.
I call that one Scarface. He weighs at least five hundred kilos.
What you see above the water is only about ten percent of him.
At 29 kilometres an hour he'll hit you like a bus with teeth.
He'll take pigs, humans and even his own hatchlings.
He can smash a fully grown cow like a tic-tac."

No one's sure if they should laugh or shit themselves.
But Ray's a friendly guy. He tells it like it is.
It comes from years of cruising this river.
He spots a yearling in mud that's invisible to us.

"I've been bitten by one that size a few times.
It feels like your finger's been hit with a hammer.
Mate, when they made the first saltwater crocodile
They got it right. No need for upgrades."

Ray says they're the psychopaths of the animal kingdom. Pure
instinct.
Remnants of a world before humans confused things.

"Ray, do you ever eat crocodiles?"

"Mate, I don't eat them and I try not to let them eat me."

Our place

We wake up to plans
undone by driving rain.
It's just like nature
to put us in our place.

A blanket left out in it
has morphed from dry to drenched.
An ageing awning
strains under water's weight.

And then a strip of blue appears
briefly in the grey.
We remake our plans
as if we have the final say.

Spider at night after rain

Air silently strums
the filaments of its home.

Night-time's music
is a humdrum symphony
of dogs, cars
and spats between cats.

The spider floats
like a seasoned acrobat
buttressed by a net
of trembling droplets.

The Commons

With errands to take care of,
I decide to walk down Church Street,
past St Stephens,
until I reach Camperdown Memorial Rest Park.
Long ago a cemetery,
it's now a place for dogs and their guardians
to move around in, to kick and throw balls:
to recreate unleashed.
One Summer
when I lived nearby,
a bunch of wags installed a couch and television
with a long extension cord
stretched from their house across the street,
and made a patch of grass a popup lounge room
where they drank boutique beers and watched footy until dark.
Green and peaceful,
it seemed a flawless snapshot of a good life.
Locals taking time to stand and chat
and pat a Labrador or Staffy.
I continue past the now
increasing glow of lights
behind curtains and blinds of semi after semi.
On reaching Salisbury I turn left
and then right at the roundabout,
progressing down Mallet
past the bowling club
now Camperdown Commons and eatery.
Lawn bowls was popular
in the suburb of my childhood.
I'd sit on a bench to watch them play
in blindingly bleached whites,

66

amused by the considered bend at the knee
before the ball was gently sent on its way to the jack.
The green was mowed and rolled so flat
it resembled pristine snooker felt.
It seemed to me a game of grace and technique
combined with a laughable absence of exertion.
Those "ladies" and "gentlemen"
could've been my grandparents.
So this is how I'll look one day I might have thought
before quickly changing tack
and careening back home
in time for mum to not panic.

       I find I've reached Parramatta Rd,
the main artery to the inner west,
the place in which I've sought refuge
for over thirty years.

       And sometimes, while reflecting
on the gilded coastal ghetto in which I came of age,
I know that this is the place that has shaped me
into the person I didn't know I'd be.

       This place of parks side by side with graffiti;
of smash repairers and neighbours in director's chairs
having drinks and snacks on footpaths;
jet engines interrupting Sunday night movies,
a place one might call the Commons, a community.

Loose ends

grey late August light
nothing is resolved
but it's fine

to leave loose ends untied
as a moth becomes manic
within the confines of this bus

self-pity is a distraction
from the action one could take
when night is now what must be faced.

A quest

"I apologise," he said
in the almost morning light.
She watched him dress and pack
for his interstate flight.

They'd performed this awkward ritual
many times before.
In the past she'd fantasized
that he'd stay to say more.

But her hope quickly dwindled.
It was hard to recall holding it.
Now she prized the time alone
which, frankly, she once feared.

She felt, not for the first time,
they'd returned to being strangers
with an ache that is pervasive
when two people were once lovers.

Then she heard him try to stop
the flyscreen door from creaking
before he sped off in a taxi
to whatever he was seeking.

Transit

She's slowly alighting
from life's relentless flight.

You know it by the way she stares
far into the distance, past trees

spattered with afternoon sunlight,
and deep through the prism of her past.

The present contains pills, glasses,
a crocheted blanket and walking frame.

Her days are sleep-filled,
punctuated with carers delivering meals

Musicians who arrive with sheets of war tunes;
brief bus outings to the seaside,

and well-meaning telephone calls
that rouse her from reveries.

In dreams there are possibilities.
There she walks and runs with ease,

visits friends and siblings
who've already passed.

In the nursing home courtyard
we laugh and banter

but time and experience
are dismantling her sentience.

These days in transit
are humdrum and precious.

Recalling kindy

an odour of sliced orange
that fresh citrus spritz
and dampness
the sludge of endless time
waiting
unable to sleep after lunch
mini dank mattresses
imprinted by small bodies
collecting priceless objects
maybe rocks or magnets
and putting them in your mouth
everything always out of reach
on high shelves
or behind locked doors.
adults' thighs at eye level
and when you graze your knees
it hurts too much
the entire world becomes pain
you search in vain for a familiar face
a voice which will embrace you
with cadences of care

Numberless hands

The psychotherapist's office door
is old and varnished to a high gloss.

From the front
you observe its dents and scratches.
From the side
you notice a panel that's crooked.

It's brass knobs have been polished
by innumerable hands.

Outside winter
is segueing into spring.
That's where you'll find sunlight,
birds and better stories.

Comfort zone

The first time he left the comfort zone
he surveyed the perimeter,
saw things that weren't familiar,
then returned to the superficial safety of his home.

The second time he left feeling slightly braver.
He ventured closer to things
he couldn't understand.
He was frightened by outsiders who looked into his eyes.
Hesitantly, he reached out his hand.

The third time he left his comfort zone
he decided to stay and camp in the unknown.
They spoke with hand gestures around a small fire.
It seemed to him that some seeds had been sown.

On the fourth he opened his home to the unknown.
He enjoyed their company.
He sensed some camaraderie.

The fifth and last time they all scoffed at the perimeter.
He and the unknown tore it down together.

When the work was done
they assessed their legacy.
They now shared a comfort zone
as far as their eyes could see.

Heimat

My Oma, whose loss and grief were immense:
a brother, a father, a homeland and hope,
chose to live a simple life:
a table, a chair, a bed and Sunlight soap

which she used for her face, and clothes and hair
in a nondescript flat for her last fifty years
sans a husband (who died young) or a dog or a cat.
Not once did I see her shed any tears.

But her love for friends and family was completely beyond question.
And there were those old sisters who lived up the road.
The all played canasta, drank coffee and spoke German,
a language which to my ears was more like a code.

And she came to our home every Friday night
to help my mother organize the Sabbath meal
which often included chopped liver and coleslaw
which we ate after saying our prayers by candlelight.

But it's been many decades since those rituals occurred.
Divorce, distance and ageing brought about their end.
Our belief in god was too weak to sustain us.
Our family's torn fabric needed many years to mend.

And my Oma, whose gains over time were immense—
a daughter, grandchildren, greatgrandchildren, and hope—
died a simple death at the age of 92.
This poem is my vain attempt at recompense.

Epigrams

1.
Those who've been and gone
never really leave.
We take them on our journey
until those who we leave grieve.

2.
When a prison door is opened
and inmates are set free
they are still imprisoned, like us all,
by life's uncertainty.

After the school fete

An empty jumping castle
deflates in waning light.

Seventh Street

Illegally parked
at Kingsford Smith Airport,

I'm slightly ill at ease
waiting for her plane to arrive.

It's almost 7pm
and Seventh Street is empty.

On my radio someone's singing,
"Should I put my faith in you?"

But that's not a question
that can ever be answered.

Sunday breakfast

Two prepubescent sons
are champing at the bit.

One look from their father
and they shrink into silence.

These parents must have been
a stunning couple once.

They still are, in their way,
though exhausted by their choices.

Strip back the affluence
and fragility's revealed.

They're all in the same boat;
Captain, First Mate and crew.

But the hierarchy will shift
before their lives are through.

Customs

Fifteen hours from Sydney's t-shirts to Dubai's flowing robes.
Its buildings are so huge they should have their own postcodes.
Hotels and the airport have dedicated prayer rooms.
It's Las Vegas's twin sans the casinos.

Our second destination is chilly Venezia.
An overcast arrival at Marco Polo airport.
Mi scusi signore, Parli inglese?
Drizzle and confusion, then we find a vaporetto.

Cruising down the Grand Canal is entering a postcard.
Wavelets jostle firmly like a hectic customs queue.
Small snowflakes twinned with rain as the day concludes
become gusts of wet ice stars blowing under umbrellas.

We emerge the next morning like newly sprouted shoots,
setting off without a map as green as aliens.
Coffee and pastry before Piazza San Marco.
We observe a toothless woman lost and laughing amongst tourists.

The second day reveals three Venetian islands.
We cram into a ferry with dozens of sightseers.
There's the customary glass blowing demo at Murano.
In waning light Burano woos us with its colours.

We cross Rialto Bridge to discover the markets.
Swordfish hacked in half and sloppy octopi.
A feeble dog scampers on a freezing concrete floor
while its botoxed owner haggles for a kilo of vongole.

Young couples nuzzle. Old men hawk hats and gloves.
The view from a bell tower gobsmacks us with charm.
Before we can pronounce acqua frizzante
we're parting with Venezia and hurtling towards Roma.

We're weary of the restrooms at shabby petrol stations
and zoom by roadside ruins on our path to Napoli.
Back in the evening we make our clumsy way
to the only laundromat within cooee of our stanza.

We drank bottles of beer
while our socks and undies tumbled.
You went off to explore.
I folded and bundled.

In my only clean t-shirt
I bought one more Peroni,
then bagged up our smalls
and walked down Via Tritone.

Athena greets us with linguistic opacity.
Its charismatic chaos is hard to resist.
Street vendors sell pastries which speak our language fluently.
Our days are stuffed full of UNESCO listed ruins.

In an ancient amphitheatre with chipped marble steps
our jaded guide details the mathematics of acoustics.
2000 B.C. walls stand without the aid of mortar.
Soon we're back on the bus and it's off to Olympia.

A delicate frost coats sacrosanct ground.
The climate and millennia have collapsed pillars like dominos.
It's impossible to winnow the truths from the myths

on a Peloponnesian morning in this past-bloated country.
N. proclaims this place is an absolute shambles.

"See, look at that idiot, he's driving down the footpath.
And that guy over there is weaving through a mall!
They become more disobedient the further south you go.
The police just loiter and smoke Marlborough.

Abandoned dogs are dumped, become wild and run free.
Here, try these potatoes and this local salami.
Have some more wine. No really, I insist.
I know Italy's corrupt, but their vice has more panache.
There's one piece of omeletta left. Don't let it go to waste!"

Early Sunday morning on Mitropoleos street.
Across from the Best Western there's a miniature Chapel.
An old man is crossing himself and kissing
what appears to me to be an illuminated manuscript.

But now it's farewell to numberless antiquities,
beauty, incompetence, Spanakopita and orange trees.
To dogs that run amok and traffic insanity.
To vromiko, koulouri and buskers with bouzoukis.

Farewell Delphi, Corinth and Olympia.
Visiting you makes one feel life should be simpler.
Farewell restored mosaics and tons of broken marble.
After a while it can start to look like rubble.

We're happy we're all healthy
but regret we're Sydney bound.
Farewell to that cabby
who broke the speed of sound.

Three observations

Late Sunday afternoon.
A fountain softly slaps itself.

*

Goldfish are a mobile
suspended in pond water.

*

A maple's star shaped leaves
are curled, arthritic hands.

Breaches

Can there be healing
from the steady accretion of breaches,
periods of silence,
moments from which you hide
and self-sooth?

What's to be done
when the sky is blue?

Can a life be retooled,
shaped like clay
still wet on a wheel?
How to stay supple.
To listen. To hear. To feel?

Home fires

She'd had enough of concealment and deception.
If it wasn't the pills, it was booze.
The cycle of recovery and bust.
Keeping the home fires burning.
The endlessly held out hope.
Tears and rage flooded the room.
The three of us were treading saltwater.
You launched empathy like a life raft.
Both of them refused to board.
She ran out brandishing car keys.
"You always leave when things get hard.
You always leave!" she wailed.
"I've told you hundreds of times not to leave."
Now it was her turn.
They turned a quiet street
into a soap opera.
"But I thought leaving would make things better,"
he squealed.
Gradually you lured them back into the building,
then into your office, then into their chairs.
"Maybe there's a third way, another path
you haven't yet travelled,"
he heard himself murmur.
"Maybe," she said.
"Maybe," he said.
There was nothing left for anyone to say.

The ocean

Many kilometres from shore
the ocean is indifferent to your fear.

There are fish that have evolved
to chew through coral.

Some can change sex
according to their school's needs.

The Maori Wrasse is known
as the puppy of the ocean.

If you wait patiently
it swims up for a pat.

But make no mistake,
the ocean will consume you.

And any proof
of your existence.

Benchmark

An elderly couple
fingers entwined
her pearl necklace
his white shirt
with singlet showing through
they are a benchmark of some kind
my gaze erases their wrinkles
liver spots and spider veins
returns them to youthfulness
the beginning of their love
which has moved incrementally
from lusting to lasting.
He says,
"I can't possibly go tonight.
my legs are aching."
And she forgives his age
as he forgives hers.

Faltenfrei

His enigmatic sepia face
dog-eared and ink stained
has travelled miles
and decades
a death which still lives
a disappearance
which seems this morning
crudely framed
his lips shine
his languid stare
with stiff white collar
tie and pocket square
this image captured
in a Viennese studio
some years before the war
his face unwrinkled seems to show
he had no clue
time was at a premium
for him and all the rest
whose lives would soon be cut
from everyone who loved them
from everyone they loved
lieber Jacob, wo bist du?

English translations from German:
Faltenfrei: Wrinkle free
lieber Jacob, wo bist du?: Dear Jacob, where are you?

For T.

Twelve years have elapsed since her body was washed up
and numbly identified. The grief was exponential.

You cried like a relative at the memorial
amongst a milling throng of love and disbelief.

Since the age of fifteen she was tortured by pain
which experts were never quite able to explain.

Love, work and hope sustained her day by day.
When they stopped working, she turned to Fentanyl.

She came to see you week after week.
Together you tried to untangle her betrayal.

"Why is all of this happening to me?"
"What made him transform from compassionate to cruel?"

You wondered the same but listened and processed.
In the silence between visits you feared for her safety.

Sometimes she'd cancel, groggy and tearful.
Mostly she turned up radiant with bravery.

On the day she didn't show you must have been busy.
Then a call from her mother let you know it was finished.

"Goodbye," the text declared with exhausted resignation.
They'd never seen concision imbued with so much gravity.

Spades

Curiosity is fragile.
Children have it in spades.

They use spades to dig,
bury treasure, build sandcastles.

There is so much we stop knowing.
A callus slowly forms.

At first, we are enmeshed
and gorge on the unknown.

Our pulses race,
but often the race ends.

The finish line is passed,
We bury our feelings.

Fragility is curious.
As grownups we have it in spades.

Newcomers

Again, you walk downhill
past each familiar house.
One where a man
emerges each morning
dressed tightly in cyclist lycra.
He watches you notice him
but never says a word.

Another where a Porsche
is always parked outside,
a pile of uncollected letters
mounting near the door.

The house of a smiling rev-head
who works on his car at weekends
and owns a pudgy French bulldog
which he takes for long walks
in the steaming mouth of winter.

The half-gutted house of a family
who live somewhere else
but are busy renovating
with the aim of renting soon.

Each day mother and son
stand outside, talking.
And sometimes it's just the daughter
who smokes and waits
for something to start or finish.

And there's the house
next door to yours
where the couple
who welcomed you to this street
once lived,
who quietly left a gift
on your front step
and helped teach you
the meaning of neighbourliness,

so that five years on
you too greet newcomers
with a gift and hopeful smile,
hope being one way
of staving off a final truth.

And tonight,
as you near your front gate,
sensor lights illuminate a path
while you fumble, as usual,
to find the right key.

Council pick-up

Momentum gathers
as the day approaches.

It's a modern-day version
of bringing out your dead.

An ominously stained mattress
leans up against a tree.

A chipped, chipboard wardrobe
swells from overnight rain.

Banana lounges continue rusting
with upholstery perished from tanning oil and sun.

There are toasters which have lost
their pop-up capability.

Fridges whose contents began to freeze
and freezers that thawed theirs.

Rice cookers which started
to run out of steam.

Cutlery and crockery
that have seen their last supper.

Bread makers which were given
as novel wedding gifts

but quickly ended up
as kitchen benchtop ornaments.

And a lone Hammond organ
as if washed ashore,

the wreckage left behind
by a 60s prog rock band

that sailed into earth, wind and fire
and sank without survivors.

Acknowledgements

ACU Poetry Prize Anthology (2018), *Coolabah 23 Anthology Universitat de Barcelona* (online), *The Blue Nib 47* (online), *The Canberra Times*, *Right Hand Pointing* (online), *Meniscus* (Volume 10, Issue 1) *Mountain Secrets Anthology* (Ginninderra Press, 2019), *Signs: The University of Canberra Vice-Chancellor's International Poetry Prize Anthology* (2018), *Wild Anthology* (Ginninderra Press, 2018),

Many thanks to David Musgrave for agreeing to publish *Trojan Gifts*. And much gratitude to Paul Kane and Adam Aitken for their kind and encouraging words and to Robert Gray for being a friend, mentor and exemplar over many years.

A special thanks to Greg McLaren for his friendship, advice and humour over the decades and for helping to edit Trojan Gifts.

As always, this book is dedicated to Lisa, Abby and Jake.